POST-HOLIDAY BLUES

Tuesday – Sunday, 11am – 8pm
T +44 (0)20 7921 0943
F +44 (0)20 7921 ̶ ̶ ̶ ̶
www.poe⁺

POETRY LIBRARY

rary housing
Collection at

HBANK
TRE

POST-HOLIDAY BLUES

Gerry Stewart

FlambardPress

First published in Great Britain in 2007 by Flambard Press
Stable Cottage, East Fourstones, Hexham NE47 5DX
www.flambardpress.co.uk

Typeset by BookType
Cover Design by Gainford Design Associates
Printed in Great Britain by Cromwell Press, Trowbridge, Wiltshire

A CIP catalogue record for this book
is available from the British Library.
ISBN 978-1-873226-92-6

Flambard Press wishes to thank Arts Council England
for its financial support.

Flambard Press is a member of Inpress,
and of Independent Northern Publishers.

Mixed Sources
Product group from well-managed
forests and other controlled sources
www.fsc.org Cert no. TT-COC-2082
© 1996 Forest Stewardship Council
FSC

For Steven
words will never be enough
and Aidan
our new life unfolding

Acknowledgements

I would like to thank all my family and friends for their support and encouragement, especially Steven who has always believed that my writing was important, even when I doubted. Thanks also to all the writers, colleagues and students I have worked with over the years, including Jen Hadfield, without whom this collection would be a shadow of its true self, and Elizabeth Reeder who has encouraged my work in all it incarnations.

Some of these poems have previously appeared in *Black Mountain Review*, *Cencrastus*, *Chapman*, *Cutting Teeth*, *Descant*, *Do Dreams Come True* anthology, *Edgz* (USA), *Envoi*, *Groundswell*, *Hanging Loose* (USA), *Iota*, *Jones Ave* (Canada), *The Journal*, *Keystone*, *Laddie*, *Lassie*, *Love* (Finland), *lichen* (Canada), *Nerve*, *The New Writer*, *New Writing Scotland 18*, *NorthWords*, *Obsessed with Pipework*, *Orbis*, *Poetry Ireland Review*, *Poetry Scotland*, *Present Poets 2* anthology, *Semicerchio* (Italy), *Sepia*, smallspiralnotebook. com and smallspiralnotebook anthology, *Smiths Knoll*, suitcasegeneration.com and *Word Jig* anthology (USA).

Contents

Untranslatable	11
Pirovolimenos	12
The Philosopher on the Beach	13
Blurred by the Sea	14
Foreign Soil	15
The Sighting	16
Windswept and Interesting	18
Sun Burnt	19
The Myth of the Expatriate	20
Inspired by Oprah	22
Flights of Fancy	23
North Wales, January 1992	24
Elsewhere	25
Post-Holiday Blues	26
Shattered Mosaics	27
Alexandrine Footnotes	28
Radio Poetry and Silence	30
Prayer	32
Deep Water	34
Italian Holiday	35
Walking Chichén Itzá	36
The Sharing of Mexico	38
Kalypso in Winter	40
Of Slugs and Green Glass	41
Jeg Skal Aldri Gråte	42
In a Stavanger Café	43
Returning to Stavanger, Norway	44
Chiselled Days in Oslo	45
L'afa e L'ombra Benedetta	46

A Woman Alone	48
Waking (Sleeping) Alone	49
The Diarist	50
Caught in an Early Spring Hail	51
The Hidden Woman	52
Waiting for Autumn	53
Breakfast Etiquette	54
inside your kiss	55
Glasgow Pub Crawl	56
Terminus	58
Regrets	59
Patterns	60
Negatives	61
Marilyn Monroe is a Rock Climber	62
Critter-Hugger	63
Beyond is the Ocean	64
Cottonwoods	65
Road Trip Not Taken	66
Reflections During a Bassline	67
Running from Darker Eyes	68
Creation Myths	69
Her Colours	70
Reminiscent House	72
Genealogy	73
Childhood Fisherman	74
You Carry Your Storms with You	75
Travelling Poems	76
A New Recipe for Dreams	77

Untranslatable

An Italian article on a Mayan volcano,
quick guttural stops, swallowed vowels:
villages lost beneath ash and fire.

Reading over your shoulder,
I pick out cognates from the swirling letters.

You travel light in this language,
confident strides, no backward glances.

*

There is safety in arguing in foreign cities.
We ruffle pigeons with our anonymous anger.

We march across squares like invading armies,
shouting while locals drink.
Old women brush by with paper bags,
their red scarves flags before us.

There is no need to explain ourselves
in the aftermath of tears and caresses.

*

You whisper a phrase in Italian,
say it is 'I love you' loosely translated.
I search the dictionary for meaning,
needing the security of solid words.

Pirovolimenos

My students ignore their lessons,
ask me to parrot in Greek,
'Good day, how are you.'
Greeted by bored faces
I shout, '*Pirovolimenos.*'
'Shot in the head,'
I translate proudly, 'crazy.'

Now lent a credibility of sorts,
they try to teach me more,
but the letters never settle in my mind.

An unmarried woman, living in a country
with no footing or friends,
crazy is the only way locals can see me.

I wander postcard vistas,
a perpetual tourist,
squinting at alien street signs,
defeated.

When my phrasebook patter runs dry
I whip out *pirovolimenos*
– a Greek supercalifragilisticexpialidocious –
just to keep them guessing.

The Philosopher on the Beach

What do you write, my lord?

Words,
       words,
              words.
This beach is too hard for anything else.
My thoughts crash like waves,
sweeping out before I can gather them up.

My students chirp around me like wild birds,
mimicking my lessons,
throwing my phrases back into my face.
See, their nimble fingers
make shadow puppets on the cave wall.

There is no corruption of these youths.
What I say to them is barren,
falling upon their minds
like the sea upon this shingle.

Beneath, thousands of years
have ground down pottery, roof tiles,
the bones of their ancestors into fine sand.
Beachcombers and their dogs brush by me,
dig through seaweed and wrack,
learning more than those dancing
beneath the burning sun.

I teach others what I cannot pass on,
a bitter poison.
I write words,
              only words into sand.

No spoon is big enough
for the gaping mouths of children.

Blurred by the Sea

We have stepped into the retelling of a myth.
Fields around the olive trees burn dry.
I ground myself in silvered, smoke-warmed leaves,
laurel and sweet almonds.

At our house built with black stones
from the imported beach,
thin-skinned grapes frame the door,
cooking perfumes the garden.

Tiny lizards scramble across the cool tiles.
Captured, they grip at your hand,
blink knowing calm eyes.

At the typewriter my eyes are dry,
unfocused with rising salt.
Finished pages are flung down
past the clock tower,
into the harbour.

Settling on the surface
above the ghosts of sunken boats
where masts stretch,
rattling like loose change.

Fishermen spread their nets to dry
in the water's reflection.
Knots fall away
like rusted lace
in the evening rain.

Trawlers and tourists' yachts
linger in the arms of sunset.

You sip cloudy ouzo,
the moon cutting a trail
as Orion cartwheels across winter.

Foreign Soil

An anchored ship. The harbour drawing away from it, then
with the force of a proffered kiss pulling it close again. She
watches the fluid motion, her breath keeping time. It is like
falling asleep with that sudden jerk back into awareness.

Waiters hourly replace her empty glass with full. Retsina
catches in her throat, an after-thought of pine forests.

She knows Odysseus once sailed these straits, searching for
his home, each island laying claim to his exploits. He landed
on these shores only last week, confides the waiter, and she
believes him.

Just as in ancient times, fishermen return, their clothes ripe
with brine. A basket handed to the kitchen staff reappears as
a plate of delicately fried fish, each smaller than a pinkie.
Sliced lemons, salad and bread follow glasses of ouzo.

As the men start eating, a foreign couple stumble to their
table behind a local man. Joking, he half-heartedly translates
for them. They laugh politely, speaking halting Greek. They
sit to eat, though the woman only picks at a bit of bread.
After a while she falls asleep against her partner's shoulder,
her hair tumbling over them.

The watcher leaves them floating at the edge of her vision,
swallows spinning amongst the clouds. She too would have
looked out of place if she had been doing anything besides
drinking. She could drink in any language.

She sees in these simple moments – a woman sleeping
beside her lover, the laughter of a communal meal – the past
resurface in the present, fresh and vibrant.

The Sighting

Orange trees flood the garden
with a heavy, unmistakable scent.

Barefoot, we watch twilight intertwine
with a storm over the bay.

The air blue, liquid.
Haze and sealight melt
until distant hills dissolve,
closing us off.

Fins of black glass cut the surface.
We chase them to the dock
as they dart beneath the rope-anchored ferries.

Soiled clothes lie abandoned
by an overturned boat.

You take pictures in the rain
as dolphins jump and twist.

On the beach gypsies sleep
to the glow of bonfires and televisions.

Gathering kindling for our own fire,
the wood is wet, the lighter burns itself out.

A night mist creeps over us
to the hiss of waves and sand.

On our return one set of footprints
remains in the stones.
I have been washed away.

Later, we will find only watery photos,
unsliced by fins.

We will send these missed chances to friends.
They say more than words
of our longing for home.

Windswept and Interesting

An odd-shaped envelope,
encumbered by stamps,
wears the scars
of the local postman's indelicate hand.

Falling grains of sand
scatter over the professor's desk.

The enclosed letter:
'Apologies for the pages' rough state,
written on a Greek beach
with a grumpy manual typewriter.'

Proofed in a walled garden,
it retains the scent of orange blossoms.

Beside cracked spines
and essays' unmarked gray wings,
the dissertation's wrappings
shake themselves loose,

fall to the floor
in an origami summer shower.

Sun Burnt

Against ancient sandstone walls
you craft our battles like Thucydides.

The yucca looms
hunched-back over the wall,
vivid, succulent flowers
hiding a subtle bite.
We take a fruit home to explore,
digging it open with a knife.
Spines catch in clothes and fingers.
For days the sharp, invisible slivers
make themselves known to our touch.

Beneath the garden umbrella
my skin glows pale
like raw, unbleached linen
while on the pebbled beach
yours has coloured,
tasting like thick sweet mocha.
You are Homer's sailor,
hair crisping with sun and salt.

Sheltered in the town's reluctant arms,
we slip like venom beneath each other's skin
until I chase you up the Venetian hill
with accusations behind my broom and duster.

We cannot live like Spartans,
poised for ambush.
We need to ease the irritation,
an abrupt downpour of tenderness
to renew tired skin.

The sky remains unbroken.

The Myth of the Expatriate

Hemingway's lost generation lived with abandon;
    in the bull-ring,
            in the alleys of Paris,
                  on safari.

They posed for artists,
began furious affairs with strangers.
Relished poverty's tattered elegance,
    scraping meals together,
            living on pennies.

Alcohol-nights,
    coffee-days,
they discharged words with machine-gun energy
        in cafés,
            dingy rooms
between lovers and adventures.

Departure dates lend passion to chance meetings.
Three weeks to discover
    every inch of a body,
four months to learn
    a city's backstreets.

I come back from work,
smelling of stale smoke and burnt meat.
Free myself from red tape
only to be caught up
    with a city,
          an undiscovered someone.

When I lose my sense of direction
I return to my notebooks
     full of addresses,
         foreign phrases,
             borrowed quotes
to retrace my steps.

Home is a furled map I sketch between
     passport stamps,
        poems,
           memories of kisses.

I chart the dangerous waters I have chosen to sail,
imagine dragons I have yet to behold.

Inspired by Oprah

Run away to the desert for forty days,
build yourself a cabin in the mountains,
take a year-long vow of silence
or climb Mount Kilimanjaro.
Rebuild your life, she suggests to the camera.

I need a sabbatical from the world.

One guest's two-week vow of silence
is already shattered by technology.
What the audience takes from the desert
is a fear of mice seeking warmth,
not the clarity found in blizzards
or the lack of human contact.

Oprah offers us the mountain,
but only holds a pebble in her hand,
swearing seven days
without a bath is unfeasible.

Only the woman living alone
near the sea revealed true wisdom.
Stomp away from those who drain our energies.

Like Shirley Valentine,
I will fill my vacant corners.
Begin by turning off the din,
starting with Oprah.

Flights of Fancy

Swallows drop from the eaves.
Envious, my breath catapults
a milk-weed parachute skywards,
releasing a wish.

With a kite's pulling string
I long to see where the wind runs,
let it tug me free of my foundations.

A child's creation
of silk and balsa wood,
a fragile hope to meet
the Earth's resistance to surrender
with my own.

Wings hum against currents,
I leapfrog into the heavens
on a dragonfly's slender back.

Beneath the stars, I dream
of slipping free of my tether of atmosphere
to dance in pure weightlessness.

North Wales, January 1992

They say the cathedral made the city.
The sea rushes to meet me,
drowning me in its language,
despite my verbal thrashings.

I can't face the castle,
under its eyes I am only a tourist.

A guidebook's sure voice cannot save me
from winter's grey smothering the city.

I struggle against it,
following bubbling umbrellas
up unnamed streets.

Walk for miles.
Mountains' cold fingers push
through dying bracken and ferns.

The road leads to warmth,
a pub and hesitating smiles.
Here winter subsides
to the glow of secrets
passed among regulars like pints.

On the train, dream-tinted postcards
increase the distance between myself
and the stamp's destination.

The absence of each foreign address
fills the empty stations as I pass.

Elsewhere

Streets maze their way
to the shop off the Rio Tera' degli Assassini.
Darkness beckons, sinking me into bliss –
leather-bound books,
handmade paper.

To the tune of muted evening,
I walk towards Dorsoduro,
the hard-backed side of the city.

The lemon bite of vaporettos.

Canals whispering
with shadowed and dampened sleep.

In my dreams the waters flow up
into the Ponte dei Sospiri,
carrying the condemned away
with the spring floods.

All I create is eaten away
by the *acqua alta*.

Emptied of resistance,
I curl around my crumbled foundations.

Serenissima.

Post-Holiday Blues

*'One always, sooner or later, comes upon a city
which is an image of one's inner cities.'*
                                    Anaïs Nin

I no longer fit into my life.
Venice has remoulded my limbs
into looped canal curves
and uncharted lagoons.

Scotland hangs off me,
a winter coat in summer,
pockets and sleeves empty.

Ballast needs to be released
and all itineraries thrown out.
Quiet streets lie unexplored.
Serenity is lost in timetables.

I want to glide, a gondola unmoored,
walk masked and unknown.

Thirty looms and the current settles,
experiences silting up.

I carry on dredging the mysterious depths.

Venice must not fade away,
like music drifting down
from shuttered rooms
onto a shadowed alley.

Caught in this Scottish deluge
I retrace her arabesques onto my skin.

Shattered Mosaics

The mask looms in the sunlit corner, its blank eyes larger
than my head. Poseidon's seaweed curls and salt beard so
fresh we feel his sea-mist hand sculpt the air between us.
Released from teaching for a long weekend, we wander
Delphi's empty ruins with off-season freedom. The winter
hours push us forward.

Beneath the watchful eye of a prowling sphinx a mosaic
glitters. Tiny stones lost, gaps in the bull's tossing head, the
lion's tail. I piece us together, stumbling over language and
tumbled emotions, unsure if we will continue to fit snugly
against each other.

We walk between this decaying world and the one we build
on shifting ground. You crawl over the barrier to taste the
sulphuric water. There is no seer to help us find the way. I
could pray for visions to guide us, but already we are blindly
planning next year.

Alexandrine Footnotes

Durrell and Cavafy seduce me
with whispered relics of Alexandria.

On each page I collide
with accents of the Orient and Levant:

lost years, illicit pleasures,
curious characters merging
with the inescapable landscape.

Silt drifts from their books,

revealing Cleopatra's submerged island
where stone priests sleep
within the hulls of iron ships.

In libraries and cafés
the city's bespectacled past lifts its head

to notice young men in cinnamon-brown suits,
unaware of the generations
that laboured beneath their feet.

Ancient kings and scholars now
forgotten by all but footnotes.

I catch the scent of orange oil
from a hidden roof garden,
the market's palette of spices.

White-needled minarets shimmer
in the moist, palpitating heat.

Their cast-off poetry washes in at my feet
with the flooding Nile,

half-phrases and rhymes,
age-broken and ground
into the smallest syllables.

The debris of mystic life captured:

dust rising in alleys,
whorls in crackled glaze
on a pot of mint tea.

Behind shuttered windows,
our skin soaks up each other
until we are one dream
of a desert's falling night.

Radio Poetry and Silence

I want you to remain
unattached, unconnected.
The night outside
the crowded radio programme
imagines us close.
Your worn silver ring floats
through the shadows of your dark hair.
Its glow on your left hand catches me,
awakening plosions from the microphone.
In a black and blue world you exist
against the force of our poetry
(teeth falling from a mouth
into a well of sacrifice).
The truth shatters the airwaves.

*

Why should your battered passport
curling on the glass counter
leave me unable to speak?
I search for reasons to follow,
even if I am the one to vanish.
My tea clouds over,
sugar dries on the tongue.
The café fills with words.
I miss you from across the room,
our moments together
projected onto a lonely dinner
on my bedroom floor.

*

I am somewhere
with no significance on your map,
distanced not only by miles, but by years.
I wait for your book to fall into my lap,
your name long on my mind.
I walk through the night
to prove to myself I am here.
I never returned to closed-eyes listening
to your midnight radio programme.

Prayer

Hanging candles swing with her whispers,
the once-reassuring prayer.

The thrum within will not let her words
reach the wide-eyed saints.

*

They walk beneath the olive trees
towards the white shrine,
coils of snakeskin shade
crawling over bark and faces.
Crossing herself she enters the cool cell.

He remains outside, smoking.
His echo moves past her
as he talks with the village children
who followed them like a pack of dogs.

How many generations of monks
in stovepipe hats and grimy black clothes
knelt in this darkness,
how many old women
prostrated themselves before this ikon
and began their penance
by sweeping dirt and refilling candles?

Their devotion had a focus
when they stepped through the door.

*

She longs for his body,
washing away the heat in the hotel shower.
Traffic raced below as they lay
on the stripped bed, lingering to touch
through the wall of humidity.

She cannot hold those memories distant here:
the rich scent of henna in her hair,
strong iced-coffee on his tongue.

*

El Greco sought escape
for an internal fire unquenched
by the stark soil of Greece.
In Spain's tossed landscape
he rediscovered his fathers' ikons;

solemn eyes, acidic thin faces
drawn up the canvas,
freed from the weight of sin.

Washed with a clear, alien light
passion pushing away the darkness.

*

She wants to be supported
by both his arms and her faith,
among the glaring eyes of these mountains.

Meld stone and flesh together.

Words do not hold the strength she needs.
She returns. For a moment,
he is lost in the sun's sharp glare.

Deep Water

Moonlight dissolves black water
as we lie on the darkened beach.
Across the shimmering harbour
the hills tuck in the village for the night.

I take off my glasses to swim,
straining to focus on your body
slipping into the sea.
We waver, free from gravity.

Struggling to remain buoyant,
I draw deep breaths.
You dive around me
like the dolphins we long to see.

Filled with lead, my limbs slow
until I lose contact with the shore.

We could have crawled
under an overturned boat,
made love like students,
listening for feet crunching on pebbles.

You could have thrown me into the sea
to celebrate the beginning of summer,
held me struggling in your arms.

Instead I flail to find sharp sand,
lie at the sea's edge gasping for air.
Sunflowers of light
explode before my eyes.

Along the promenade
locals don't notice
when you carry me home.

Italian Holiday

'Do you want an Italian *amante*?'
asked the man at the Hotel Adria.
After the cool rain he smothers me
in the richness of his cigarettes and coffee.

The streets are white-washed canyons of laundry
protected by plastic rain sheets.
Shrines full of wilted flowers and candle wax
mark every corner with gilt stares.

A woman motions to me from a silent entry.
'Avoid the old city,' she warns.

Where did the two cities part, the way unmarked
by surrounding walls or signposts?

My missed boat glides beyond the citadel.

Greek visa expired,
I sailed two days from comfortable arms.
My lover left behind among ripe lemon trees.

I imagine myself sleeping
in the shelter of courtyard stairs,
open to the rain, away from wind and traffic.

Lovers climb above me, returning from late theatre,
their laughter falling into puddles.
Whispers brush like a kiss at the base of my neck.

I am caught in this country,
dragged in rough circles through choked streets,
counting the hours to my departure.

The wrought-iron lift
grates in the heart of the hotel
throughout the night.

Walking Chichén Itzá

I breathe the same air
she once did
looking to her gods in treetop heavens

those faces carved in stone
found still in men and boys
selling water and trinkets
at the jungle's edge

I walk down roads dust-red
past the gates of cool hotels

a quetzal's green wings
emerge from her back
lifting her above
cameras and tour guides

her ancient spirit burns through
circles the unearthed mounds
to reveal the snake they once held
coiled around the trees' silence

a white temple lost in deep growth
roughened by rains reappears
jaguars and warriors
form from mist to bow before her

she throws her soul back
to the darkening night cries

did they toss her fighting
into the sinking cenote?
she would float
fingering brown waves
face turned to the sun
laughing as it called for her death

did she speak to her feathered gods
bringing their words of light
back to her people with a shallow breath?

she breathes now
opening frayed doors
imprinted within her

and I pass through
to the pyramid's heights
foreign voices falling below
grasping for stones
of the way she once knew

Chichén Itzá is a Mexican Mayan site. Cenotes are sinkholes that were used as wells and also as holy sites. Sacrificial victims were thrown in and if they survived became messengers of the gods.

The Sharing of Mexico

Her mind unfolds, a dark ribbon
awakening under market tents.
She sits rearranged like her rugs,
spread out to catch the eye.
Her earth-skin reflects
the horizon-shaking heat.

She no longer sees pesos
pressed into her cool palm
or children running up to dusty cars,
offering smiles,
shrivelled *naranjas*.

The ribbon leads her away,
to the corrugated tin of her shack,
mud flowing in red trails beneath bare feet,
frying food and sweet sleep.

Above her the canopy sighs,
encouraging the heavy wind to grasp
the flat grey-yellow land and her sun.

She repeats her name, Caribe,
colours worked in rough wool.
She strokes her pale grey, pink,
peach of stucco,
the smooth blue of hanging water,
the lost green of distant jungle.

She strains to share more than words.
A hope of afternoon rain collects
around broad-leaved flowers.

Her voice echoes out to tourists,
passing from her stall to white hotel rooms,
slow fans churning the moist air.

Llueve, she says, it is raining.

Kalypso in Winter

Since you sailed
storms have dredged up my shore.

Waves pound through me like an irregular drum.

I long to take up the beat, to call you back,
batter down these echoing cliffs
and run the seabed to your side.

Can you feel my urgency
as you walk your stony island?

Your hearth is crowded with songs and laughter,
yet your brow is furrowed with unsaid words.

I pitch my tears into clouds
to be carried away by flocks of seagulls.

If I wrapped you in my cloak of spells
would you talk yourself free
or fly away on your ship's wings?

You will return to my isle without tricks,
your eyes will not drift homeward.

I send you my love
like a cold-sea kiss upon your wrist.

Of Slugs and Green Glass

I escape mornings in the waking house.
Slugs crawl from beneath wet bushes,
only to be crushed underfoot before the sun rises.
At the bus stop I memorise puddles,
reflecting the grey sky.

Posters on the red-brick wall
are torn reminders of discos
and slow dancing I missed.

The bus door cries open,
braking against crushed green glass,
as the students rush in.
I hide down in dusty leather seats.

Crumbling stone walls stretch out to the sea.
The bus follows a different route every day,
yet no one is left behind.

Day arrives late as we step off in town.
At the pond swans fight for bread.
Classes have started, I crunch gravel
and broken glass under my feet.

Jeg Skal Aldri Gråte

(I Shall Never Cry)

The sun fades
over the lightly sketched
Norwegian landscape.
I am alone, walking along
shadows of stone walls.

Here, the rain running in streams
over dark earth can be my language.
Hay threshers, caught like dinosaurs
in the clear ice-sky,
wait with me for the return of the sun.

Beyond these empty fields
lies a house with closed faces
and the endless muted blues
of horizon and sea.
I move back into the shelter
of stone-hard hills.

In a Stavanger Café

Abandoning the dark cloak of the storm,
she fades into the waiting café.
Candles flicker to a jungle beat.
The white king serves the tea,
braiding ceiling nudes with the chequered floor.

She has fallen down no rabbit hole,
just the stairs of the tower
hanging over the town,
its sleepy rain-cloud eyes closed.

Fairy-tale characters come in and out,
laughing and calling.
The immortal Caesar curled in his corner niche
smiles like that English county cat.
Sharp tongues purr fluent language.

She tries to predict her future
in a cup of raspberry tea, but the leaves blur.
Voices rise, creep in with the opening door,
fighting the flow of music.

Outside all is swept clean by the wind.
It ushers her out beneath dull street-lights,
into the city's arms at long last.

Returning to Stavanger, Norway

for Elisabeth

Even after absence I had hoped
the narrow winding cobbled alleys
would remain unchanged.

On this corner, a man sang
to a battered guitar until our coins flashed
dully into his green felt hat.

Miracles were proclaimed in shop windows;
'If not here, find it inside.'

I remember the cannons,
the spray-painted copper woman:
days we slow danced with these crowds.

As I walk, the fish market
hangs evening from its shutters.
Empty piers are smeared with shadows
like photos faded to yellow age.
There is no city without your guiding hand.

Cinemas and glass buildings block the sea.
Climbing the hill to our black and white café,
faces inside have woken to unexpected youth.

The familiar statues are gone
and they no longer carry my favourite tea.

But you tell me the girls walk
arm-in-arm just as we did
and men still sing on late-night buses.
They continue on as if the sea's violent tug
will never wear away the land.

Chiselled Days in Oslo

for Fredrik

We are both teething on this city of statues.
Salty-sweet from the fjord's interruption,
she catches me by surprise.

Her toes baked with sand,
her whip-whistle sky shakes away
my memories of rain-wet stone
and a mouthful of pebbles.

Water baby curled in your plastic womb,
your legs stretch ready to launch you
from infancy's lukewarm waves.
Your laughing face reprimands my granite child,
clenched into an eternal grimace.

We tumble like autumn leaves over pools
of polar bears and stiff-suited politicians.
Their bodies bend in celebration of your first summer,
exiting without a clumsy end.
Their mineral arms wait to embrace your first steps.

L'afa e L'ombra Benedetta

(Sultry Heat and Blessed Shade)

'Henceforward in thy shadow. Nevermore . . . Serenely in the sunshine as before.'
    Elizabeth Barrett Browning, *Sonnets from the Portuguese*

The discarded hotel flickers in the heat,
having made the difficult translation
into elegant neglect.
A burnt white radiance
against the overhanging trees.

I imagine the dark Portuguese
pacing her restless sonnets
behind broken-in windows.

I stumble, exposed
in the presence of her serenity.

Over the hills echoes
the café Englishman's mouth,
shouting her myth in rattling Italian.

Those muddied words slip
from holes in my pockets
along with the stones of my poetry.

Flowered Catherine-wheels crackle
from terracotta roof tiles.
Her fingertips trail crushed rosemary
down to my humbled road.

Her phrased shade falls
like a blessed kiss,
cooling the sting of summer salt
between my shoulder blades.

Before I can taste its sultry hint,
it evaporates to a whisper.

The 'dark Portuguese' in my poem and EBB's Sonnets refers to
Robert Browning describing his wife in this way because of her
colouring. Her Sonnets are not translated from Portuguese as is
often thought.

A Woman Alone

After reading Elizabeth Bishop

She finds balance in maps,
small geographies unwound.
Their pliant contours are translated
like an ancient language
when travelled by the simplest means.

She wrote to the hum
of mosquitoes and museums.
Now, older, to paint
fading on the front porch.

She cannot release her birth-accent
wrapped around her like an uncut cord.

She could tell you of being detained in Brazil
by the unripe fruit of the almond,
about baseball or a little girl scribbling away,
her voice a gentle caress.

Her stories like her lovers are anonymous
in the crackle of static electricity surrounding her.

She draws us to her like moths to the moon
and repels our advances with the same mask.

Waking (Sleeping) Alone

Two nights she has crawled out of his arms,
hid in a candle, a book, a glass of water.
All just words to escape his voice,
dark against the orange sky.

She wrote the words on the sheets,
hoping they wouldn't wash out.
If she cried them away
their ghosts would remain
smeared against her cheek, tangled in her hair.

During the day she felt devil's knots at her scalp,
caught their scent in her movements.
She feels unrooted without his body next to hers.

Tonight, she will shut out the night,
fold up into herself, to dream of the safer unknown.
Wine sours on the table,
the large space in the bed is imagined.
Sleep enters no easier past empty arms.

The Diarist

My tears and laughter fall hard onto paper
where I share these hectic moments:
your intensities I must scratch out
and bind in plain words to understand.

Metaphors of fear and exposure appear,
first discovered in the handwriting of your skin.
My emotions lie buried in this vaulted cave
and through you I view its darkest corners.

The words I give you are borrowed;
drifting conversations, lines from favourite books.
I know you fear my silent hours
when I pick up the pen-knife
that cuts our time together into digestible
but unrecognisable sentences.

As I lay my journal down I see your eyes,
wondering if I am the same woman
who raged with fire and wept seas in your arms.

How much do I soak up through open pores,
how much blood does my pen lace across the page?

Caught in an Early Spring Hail

Years from now I will remember you
caught in a swirl of beer, cigarettes and euphoria.

I will not need to wade back
into notes on the margins of textbooks
or old photographs to find you.

Icicles crash onto the campus green.

You will not settle at the back of my mind.
I resist the pressing thought
that you might hear me
whispering through the storm
and pull me through.

I have turned to the light of your window,
not knowing what I wanted to see.
If you were there I would disappear, dust in the air.

Can I spare the world, not knowing
what strange luck April holds for me?

The hail continues to fall.
I cannot breathe beneath its weight
or lift my eyes and smile
in this cold world that falls around me.

The Hidden Woman

Morning finds a woman's love
trapped in clear amber.

Her house is strangely calm in his absence.
Buoyed by the spice of naked skin,
she folds their muffled thunder into sheets,
sweeps the wine and musk evenings under rugs.
The room conceals their music in the walls.

On her wrist he has left one evergreen kiss
to remember in bank queues, on crowded buses.

She does not waver
beneath neighbours' gaunt scarecrow eyes.
Their dry accents rattle
against flickering sunflower curtains.

Her wet lips uncompose
their laughter as she waits
for the night's storms and caresses.

Waiting for Autumn

Her creased hands rolling dough
onto the wooden table show the years.
She prefers working oil into his burnt-brown back
until his sighs melt her aching joints.

He sneaks into the kitchen, slips his arms around her.
Spent years return in a fervour of warm tumblings.
She shrugs him off, strains her sight into the glare.

In the courtyard her children unload.
Here to visit her, they rush to the sea,
kisses thrown over their shoulders.
They avoid him, turn their noses up
at the 'exotic' meals she creates.

Two months and the winds will pick up,
gather them like leaves and rubbish
until her home is returned clean, cool and white.

Then the days will be glossy,
thick as orange leaves.
He will hold her hand in cafés,
study the cracked skin and scars.
They will buy food from street markets
and sweep away scorpions seeking their warmth.
Alone, they will hibernate.

She cooks her emotions into simple meals –
heavy soups, salads and nut breads.
The simple pleasure of watching him eat.

Breakfast Etiquette

I lace my cereal with sugar.
'You should change your eating habits,'
he says as he flicks the paper to a new page.

A cough growing from a tickle to be stifled.
I used to eat granola full of fresh fruit,
skimmed milk with seven-grain toast.
The expected is dry,
brittle as twigs underfoot.

Now I feed my body's cravings,
make late-night runs for ice cream,
swirl sweet skin around my teeth.

Feel the tingle of each kiss
served in a warm bed.

I want sex mixed
with sunlight on tousled sheets,
not the bite of toothpaste and after-shave
over the morning news.

Tomorrow's breakfast
will be muffins and hot chocolate
brought to his sleeping side.

I will cover his body with mine
until the sugar wakes him
and he searches for my arms.

He will demand all the luxuries
he has denied himself.
I will change his eating habits.

inside your kiss

the colour of dark sand
your skin tightens over muscles
I am learning the feel of my own body
to walk in the comfort
of its flow and shape
we fit

I know I can crawl
into the curve of your back
the space behind your knees
the hollow at your throat
I alone know the tiny wings
emerging from your shoulders

at night it is your breath
whispering against my neck
you wake me when I walk away
words are basic next to touch
these are pale

you grow deep in me
as I fall inside your kiss

Glasgow Pub Crawl

each street staggers
against the weight of repairs
buildings lean on scaffolding
           we duck without noticing

'dae ye hiv ony coapers, jimmy'
go on, don't stop, say no
           but you rummage
           in frayed pocket
           check for change

start at Brahms and Liszt
below street level
across from the cinema
lines stretch around the block

people outlined
shy and singing
darker on dark
everywhere close and safe

I have tasted so many whiskies
blends and malts
but still don't know
which to mix or take straight

           faces greet you
I separate
      those to be blended
      those to stand on their own

      at the Scotia the pounding blues repeat
haunting me
           you can't remember the song

with the flatcaps at the Horseshoe
as football flits over the telly
                    no one is watching
                    but when someone scores
                    we all cheer

I fall back
on my warm wooden barstool
I want to be supported

                    we start out on a crawl
          but always return to the familiar
          Students' Union
I grasp for
          the shine of metal railings
          a music half-heard

          we run into the same people
          laugh at the same jokes

          the city waits outside
          below the evening clean
                    you don't see
                    but stands forever yours

          'finish your drinks
          and make your way outside, please'
          pubs empty
          sky clears
          the Clyde pushes at the bridges
                    a river widened for us

                    we move uncertain of direction
I don't want to decide anymore
                    if you can't stay
don't tell me

                    just walk me back
                    just walk me back

Terminus

Taxis snap the thread
between us.

The street below
moves by in accents
of this room's bitter sigh.

Leaves falling
from the climbing ivy,
red teardrops.

Forward is a slap,
a pool of dirty water
that once held
a piece of the moon.

I wade into absence,
retracing mazes in coffee grounds,
unwashed dishes.

Hours of sleepy, rain-filled jazz,
broken in the confusion
of being whole and alone
between the sheets.

Nina Simone lulls me past sleep,
'I want something to live for, someone . . .'
I dream of smoke-filled rooms,
shoulders to soak up my tears.

Regrets

Starting over would be easier if I hated you.

End all memories with a slamming door,
binding you in heavy wood.
I'd listen to you pound and walk away.

I would hang green silk curtains
that crackled in the wind,
draw pictures on the ceiling with broken crayons
of the Furies dressed in garlands and fire.

I'd write you out of character
in my mind, in my poetry
to secure the distance between us.

I'd leave myself no way to step back.
My room would stand empty
to fill with scented candles, new books.

The shadows playing against my walls
would no longer wake me,
wondering if you had returned.

I'd sleep until I knew I was alone.

Patterns

Where the sun breaks a crack in the curtains
she follows a trail of silver dust to the bed.

She wants to rearrange, to feel
the heaviness of her body clearing the sheets' surface,
free herself of his burning arm thrown over her back.

The tulip on the dresser drops
a curling yellow petal onto shadowed carpet.

If she moves in moments so slow not to wake him,
she can leave the dark room,
cool air pouring against her, bracing the skin.

The kitchen clock, reciting precious seconds,
echoes within her shell of solitude.

A spider restless in the corner,
knits its web from one paper flower to the next,
dividing the shadow with thin filaments.

The house shakes loose in a long tremor,
waking sudden whispers from the oak tree against it.

The alarm shatters. He is carved from sleep.
She draws the curtains,
gazing out the clear window cascaded with light.

Negatives

The black-and-white highway
slides beneath the car,
leading to a horizon
of fields and lazy river towns.
She follows limestone cliff walls,
rising above her,
attempting to cut off escape.

Rain slashing against glass,
the torn road turns out
into squares of a rural patchwork.
The stitching is left unfinished,
threads hang loose.

Empty mornings have caught against her,
pieces of conversation forced together
until they are crushed
like eggshells into the trash.

She wants to press herself
into rows of drying corn.
Continue to the boundary woods,
until she is a flashing blur
in the glint of sun.

She turns farther away,
no sound forming under her
on the rain-softened interstate.

Marilyn Monroe is a Rock Climber

The rock face stands before her.
With one finger, she pulls herself blindly up,
tensed against the weight of watching eyes.

Marilyn with painted-loose smile,
lost herself on the glossy pages.
Open to the world, her beauty was born
from images others shaped.

A love for the mountain
moves her to attempt this.
She feels its edges meld
with her own curves,
presses forward to become stone.

We stand below, envious of her grace
as she is freed from the earth's flatness.

Critter-Hugger

My first day of hands-on I ride
a bumping pickup
into the blasted landscape.
Hours of waiting,
coffee thermosed, for a glimpse.

They arrive from the mist-sleeping woods.
Elk nudge by, two at a time,
their eyes empty of my existence.
I count racks: bone antlers
pushing wide the clearing,
three's average, six's a prize.

I ache at their stilled grace.

A black bear lolls on the road's edge,
its dry nose as wide as my fist.
Muscled limbs could shatter bone,
but it leaves as subdued as it came.

A puma's wide-padded paws trail dust.
Sandstone fur against dying grass.
I resist dipping my hand into the blood-marred pelt.

I am here to take notes,
log numbers, radio collars.

Don't ask questions of men,
lips bulged with tobacco,
eyes glazed and loose with excitement.

I perch over a black widow's web,
the hunter's station at its centre.

Cities emptied, the mountains wake
gun-speckled with neon orange.
They take their quota of kills the law allows.

Beyond is the Ocean

Her fingers brush over the white peaches.
Pared open, the flesh is rotted brown and soft.
She leaves them on the table,
a spoiled still life, turns to listen to the sea.

He found her swimming
against the iron seaweed of the bar,
an angelfish among the drowning.
He built a sturdy bed to contain
the raw-boned girl
whose hips jutted out like fins.

Love for this distant man softened her steps
until she no longer seemed out of place on land.
She recalls the symphony of their skin,
but the tide continues to pull.

She traces lines on a creased map
as if they were veins,
following the route her blood
takes away from him.

She vows one day to return to the sea
and take up her cast-off beauty.
The peach trees in the garden sway
beneath the weight of ripening fruit
caught in the sea wind.

Cottonwoods

As a child he woke
and believed the cotton was snow
beneath the thin trees.

He catches it, rolls it
between his callused fingers.
The white shrinks, hard and grey.
The rain and cotton fall.

She wants to gather the fluff in handfuls,
spin it into soft yarn or thread.
Wear it against her skin as she walks
through fields towards him.

She gets off the porch,
leaves the lights dimmed,
walks through the shadow boxes
and suitcases held together with tape.

She wants it to rain when she leaves.
It is easier to disappear in rain.
And for the full moon to stroke his cheek
at night after she is gone.

Road Trip Not Taken

Words unsaid, my rear-view mirror leaves you
engulfed in a dust-filled alleyway.

This is the trip we planned for that summer.
My little car grudgingly heaved itself
over the unlit highways of the Pacific Northwest.
We made love in rain-covered wheat fields,
stayed near the sea, climbed
fire-watchers' towers to see over the mist.
Ahead the moon was only half-formed.

As the end neared emptiness clamped down
like a bright bowl scraped clean.
Clouds hung, dark ellipses between our hesitations
as we swung under an off-ramp
and headed our separate ways.

Reflections During a Bassline

He offered to cut out my heart
and pull it from my ribcage through a slit
just above the breast he lay against.

The lights spun around the room
like water in a fishbowl.
I was growing too big,
swirling around with rusty scales.
I would soon jump out and travel
past castles not made of plastic.

I wanted to be corrupted,
to lose myself on the edge of his solo,
watching shadow girls dance on the wall.
Heads down, braceleted in silver
they wrapped their uncombed hair around me
in loose knots and pulled me forward.
The bass's throb fell from the air as if it were bronzed.
I stroked it purring around my knees.

I wanted to sleep against the stretch of his back.
Under the string of lights he held only himself
while the music buried me in heavy sand,
his face in my hair, smelling the lacing
of salt, sex and hash.

I rewrote all the stutters and silences
in the morning as I walked home –
no red carpet laid out down the alley.

Didn't he know my heart was already gone
from the place he reached into?

Running from Darker Eyes

for Scott

'You have to expect trouble with green eyes.'
His carried a wolf's knowledge of traps,
exposing the wounds she tried to protect.
Others refused to see below her calm surface.

She hid behind her glasses for years
while cities moved by in stretched-out blurs.
She found it hard to believe an escape existed.
He unfolded the map with just a smile.

She thought her eyes were like marbles,
yellowed with age. A friend said cat's eyes,
a lover had called them elven.
She saw only purple shadows beneath them.

Her emotions echoed out in pubs
and on midnight streets she couldn't run down.

On the subway home, she returned to tears.
She wrote down her origins.
A slip of paper marked the day.

Creation Myths

She begins our story
by lifting the book to her lap.

Time stills.

Grains of the page shift,
allowing her to extract an image.
We jump into the open,
baring our teeth with primal thirst.

Our moments fall from her mouth,
prancing like lost mythical beasts.
We run, satyr and naiad,
through flaking chiaroscuro courtyards
and ruined temples.
In slow embraces we find wine
and wild-smoke to entertain us.

She captures us in an amber hourglass
so she may weave our tale
for another thousand nights
until I am the sleepless girl at your feet

whispering into eternity

Her Colours

She recites her mantra over your sleep,
'Vitality defined, vital.'
She'd like to braid her chain-strong hair around you,
yet you know only my undemanding fingers.

Your touch, she announces, leaves trails
of fire engine red and iris blue.

She's hidden you in all her paintings,
peeking around a corner,
curled in the loose sheets,
never in shadows.

She constructs you
of reflected light and curving muscles.

In the painting of our street
you stare down from the elm tree,
like a spirit of the forest.

It hides me beneath yellow, burning leaves,
yet you lie untouched.

She takes you from steel-grey highrises,
burns you into long beaches –
too green for sand,
too quicksilver for water.

I can't draw you over any other background.

I want to see you
with her grape leaves in your hair,
wood-warm skin against my cheek.
I don't possess her palette.

Imagine us framed by a flat orange window.
She is the gold flash of a dark-eyed oriole,
you are the kite tugging against its tail,
while I stand in the foreground
real and close-up.

Reminiscent House

Fragments remain.

They confront her in the yard,
on bookshelves and take the shape
of ticket stubs, faint stains on jackets
packed away in dank cupboards.

The laughlines he traced pull themselves tight.
His distant fingers break into her thoughts.
She tries to paint them away in the cold hours.
The jar holding her brushes once was filled
with bitter olives they brought from Greece.

In the tub, she burns pictures of them together,
brown ashes clinging to her wet skin.
She douses the flames, cooling her throbbing limbs.
Bubbles crawl up her back and neck, through her hair.

Even her plants are descended from his.
She stands before the mirror,
pulling out ragged, silver hairs
surrounded by their fragile branches.

She never waters them. They struggle on,
soaking up mist and her half-conversations.
Leaves fall away, but new ones surprise her
in the morning, gripping her face.

Not quite dead, only lingering on
like smoke over an empty pool.

Genealogy

Until I left the Midwest
the tales were never questioned.

Great-grandfather's rumours of our family –
horse-thieves
and an old man with no birthplace.

We may be descendents
of an island man and woman fighting the elements
or the illegitimate children of kings.

I settle into Glasgow's streets,
create a language of my own.
I relearn the vowels of our surname
and find history in deaths and births.

Patterns emerge, offering few clues;
son after son not speaking to father,
the long noses and silent women.

I return without map or compass.

Childhood Fisherman

The only fisherman I ever knew
prepared his fishing floats
under watercolour ripples of shade.

Brown Mississippi flowed by.
I'd sit at his worktable under the oak tree,
as he threaded the black crickets onto hooks.

He caught them between missing fingers.
They hung down, marionettes
dancing beneath the waves.

I made mud pots on a brick wall,
filled the long hours during boat races,
wading the crowded shore.
I played in overgrown lots of violets and dust.
The Fourth lasted for a week,
the days lingered past darkness.

I had forgotten it all
until I saw a man in the bookstore
looking for a book on wildflowers.
He was weathered like my river,
missing a finger like my fisherman.

The sun returned to slide over me
as I dreamed of fossils
found in limestone on the Fourth of July,
dark water cool on my splashing feet.

You Carry Your Storms with You

When it rains Norwegian cities become slick and shiny
like fish scales or reflections on oil-covered water.
Their features merge into hazy memory
as I crawl free from the fog moving off the sea.

In Glasgow the stone takes on a softness.
Colours deepen out of the grey – gold, brick red,
deep mossy green – surfacing like leaves on a pond.
I blossom in this half-light, casting my own phosphorescence.

The winter sky in Greece opens without warning,
flooding the streets. As the sun struggles through
the air wears a blue heaviness thick enough to swim in.
The heat loosens my body until I have no boundaries.

During childhood storms I counted the miles
between lightning and thunder. The landscape's shadows
and ghosts still filter through my dreams.
I can close my eyes and slip into this safety net.

In Idaho I made love to the patter of raindrops
on a tin caravan roof. The mountains that surrounded me
like a embrace were lost in the thrill of distant clouds.
I form my myths from the valley of ripples and stone.

The rain copies your touch along my face. I reveal
these storms until you know every tree I have shaken
free of its droplets, every city I have glimpsed.

Travelling Poems

My poems live in cities I have abandoned.
They wander new streets,
eat in my favourite cafés,
drag their hands through waves
and stroke poppies growing in decaying walls.

They walk away as soon as
they discover their legs are fit for roaming.
They steal my maps and journals,
find my special corners,
swearing they cannot stay
cooped-up in this flat any longer.

My poems write me notes
on bright stiff paper and scenic postcards.
It is never what they expected.
Sometimes they are in love
and their handwriting falls along the page
like a lover's curls.
Other times they are homesick,
the food is terrible
and they would kill to hear
a single word of English.

But they won't come home.
I cheer them up by saying
it's still raining here,
the drug dealer next door
locked his wife out until the police arrived,
my friends and I are still looking
for that elusive perfect job

and another poem has left
to tramp the jungles of Mexico.

A New Recipe for Dreams

Spring arrives with muddy paws.
Dreaming of Umbria again,
spices of rich earth,
heavy clay thrown on a wheel.

I transplant a pot of basil,
black mulch slips beneath
fingernails and onto the counter,
a sprinkling of peppercorns.
A tail flicked among the leaves
seasons the coppered room.

I oil the new dead-grey pan,
feed the metal's greed.
In a low oven it ages,
glowing dark as a salamander.
Water rings off the edges.
Fired black swallows rust,
holds olive oil in its dim eye.

My cookbook is a torn jumble
of hand-written pages,
stiffened with splashes and drips.
Eat pasta for the blood.
Balance the summer presence of eggs
against snowdrifts of flour.
Working a rhythm to drive away frustration,
I roll out ribbons, quills and butterflies.

Sausages snap
against heat-seasoned cast iron,
whiskers twitching.
My mezzaluná rips herbs
into scented shreds.
The sauce sings warm notes
of roasted garlic and peppers.

We eat in the doorway,
talking of a finished garden.
You have to stand still, I warn,
to see emerging grass,
transparent sprouts
on bare blueberry bushes.

The sun is a wasp
buzzing against the window.

Spring arrives with muddy paws.